MW00425016

For more information and resources, visit dmmfbook.com.

I'll do anything, just...

DON'T MAKE ME FUND- RAISE

A GUIDE FOR RELUCTANT FUNDRAISING VOLUNTEERS

———————

ELOISE BRICE

COPYRIGHT

DEDICATION

To my wonderful children,
Jennifer and Robert

TABLE OF CONTENTS

ACKNOWLEDGMENTS

This is a book that wrote itself in some ways and over many years. From an early age, my parents were pivotal in leading me to this vocation. My father, a brilliant academic in his own right, instilled in me the belief that institutions of higher learning allow almost infinite opportunities to so many Americans and citizens from around the world. My mother was a tireless volunteer; I grew up delivering Meals on Wheels with her, observing her work with autistic children and their families, and watching her take on all sorts of causes to help our community. Together, they fueled my passion for philanthropy in higher education and were role models in the art of fundraising.

I am grateful to those who have mentored me along the way, including my first boss in fundraising, Larry Beaulaurier, Vice President for Development and Alumni Relations at Whitman College, who was an early pioneer in the new profession of fundraising.

Thanks to the many donors who have schooled me their decision-making process and the many volunteers who have been my partners over the years. This book wouldn't have been the same without you.

I am especially grateful to Rod Kirsch, who has been kind enough to counsel me over the years and also write the foreword to this book.

Thank you to those who reviewed the manuscript and provided comments from their vastly different perspectives, all expert practitioners in this field: Marybeth Brown, Rebecca Gentry, Sheila Heimbinder, Nancy Levicki, Vicki Riedel, and Richard Yankwich.

Special thanks to my husband, Steve Brice, and my children, Robert and Jennifer, whose wisdom, logical minds, and sense of humor helped me complete this book.

FOREWORD

"I'll do anything for your organization, but please don't make me fundraise!"

How many times have these words come forth as you are being asked to join the board of a non-profit?

As a volunteer, you have great enthusiasm for a cause close to your heart. You've been a generous donor. You are willing to be on the board, but the executive director wants you to help raise money. What should I say? What questions should I ask first? Could I ever possibly ask someone for money? And where do I go for help?

Now, finally, a refreshing, succinct, instructive primer is available to help you past the hurdle of asking others to give to a cause in which you believe. In Don't Make Me Fundraise!, Eloise Brice gives every volunteer the background, knowledge and confidence needed to be a successful fundraising volunteer. Brice has provided an insightful road-map for every volunteer, regardless of past experience. Included in her treatise are the behaviors of successful fundraising volunteers, the expectations of the non-profit and of you in this relationship, and the ultimate joy of seeking philanthropic investments from others who share your passion for the same cause.

Why is the skill to fundraise as a volunteer so important? Why can't the world simply afford for you to stay on the sidelines? First, we often sell ourselves and the influence we have with others short. Your presence and voice as a volunteer fundraiser can make an extraordinary difference in the success of a non-profit. You actually have a platform much more powerful than staff. Second, my observation as a fundraising executive, consultant and volunteer over four decades tells me that the highest performing and most effective non-profits have a strong cadre of fundraising volunteers to advance their missions. And finally, with over 1 million non-profits in the USA, the opportunities to improve the quality of life for others is abundant. Your involvement is urgently desired. Most non-profits don't expect perfection; they just want you to try to do your best. Brice's book gives you the right information to send you on the road to success.

I have known Eloise Brice for nearly 25 years and hold her in high esteem. She knows of what she writes. She has held executive leadership roles in higher education, healthcare and NGOs, responsible for raising billions of dollars. Prior to her significant accomplishments in leading the University of Houston as Vice Chancellor for Advancement well beyond its $1 billion campaign goal, she's also been in the trenches as a volunteer herself. She draws upon her experiences as a board member for the Eugene (OR) United Way Foundation, the board of the Central

Pennsylvania Community Foundation (PA), the board of All About Women (TN), and the Executive Women's Partnership Committee (Houston). At each non-profit she was engaged as volunteer fundraiser.

Her professional experience is equally impressive. She's served as Executive Director of the University of Oregon Foundation, Executive Director of University Development at Penn State University, Associate Vice Chancellor at Vanderbilt University and Vice President for the Children's Healthcare of Atlanta. And in between these various assignments she served as Vice President and managing director for an international consulting firm, advising presidents, boards and vice presidents on the raising of millions of dollars and the recruitment of armies of volunteers. She represents the best in philanthropic leadership.

Now, a few words to those executives who lead and manage non-profits. First, thank you for what you do to advance our society. You are indispensable. Next, I am guessing you've heard more times than you care to count, the title words of this book. The next time one of your current or potential volunteers speaks them, you now have the means to put them at ease and show them you care by placing this book in the hands of every individual on your board. What a nice gift for their service this would be.

Alexis de Tocqueville wrote *Democracy in America* after touring our young country in the 1830s. He eloquently described the power and ubiquity of volunteerism in America. He poignantly states, "The health of a democratic society may be measured by the quality of functions performed by private citizens." How very true. *Don't Make Me Fundraise!* is just one more means to heighten the transformational impact of volunteers and our collective impact on society.

Rodney P. Kirsch
Senior Vice President, Emeritus
Development and Alumni Relations
The Pennsylvania State University

"The raising of extraordinarily large sums of money, given voluntarily and freely by millions of our fellow citizens, is uniquely American and it represents the best of American tradition."
—John F. Kennedy

INTRODUCTION

LIKE SO MANY, MY FUNDRAISING JOURNEY BEGAN BY selling Girl Scout cookies. I was diligent but not motivated by the money itself, winning all the awards, or becoming a top-seller. I was motivated by the cookies. I knew at the end, there was a box of Samoas waiting for me. To my 10 year-old brain, the cookies were synonymous with the mission. They were both the goal and the reward.

Over the years, I've served on non-profit boards, community foundation boards, and been a staff leader in major campaigns; and this fundamental truth about myself has not changed: I'm still motivated by the cookie — the ultimate goal of the campaign. Whether it's a new gym, annual budget, endowment, or capital campaign, the positive change in my community and opportunities for humanity are the forces that move me forward. And each step along the way, volunteers have been a key ingredient to every success I've attained.

I joined the University of Houston (UH) System in 2012 as Vice Chancellor for Advancement. Responsible for alumni relations, fundraising, and volunteer engagement while serving as a member of the President's Cabinet, I lead an organization of 160 employees and coordinate all fundraising for the UH System and all its campuses with annual private support of over $200 million last year.

Under my leadership, the UH System launched a $1 billion fundraising campaign, the University's first comprehensive campaign in a quarter century. As I write this, our "Here, We Go" Campaign has raised over $1 billion, 18 months ahead of schedule.

This achievement would not have been possible had I not marshaled a small army of volunteer advocates. This team consisted of UH's advisory committee, the Board of Visitors, and a high-profile Campaign Executive Committee, consisting of some of Houston's most prominent leaders to advise on campaign strategy, and hundreds of other campaign volunteers.

We hadn't had a campaign for 25 years, and we didn't have any fundraising volunteers, though we did have plenty of wonderful alumni and friends. I was reminded just how powerful passion and an engaged team of volunteer partners could be. I simply could not have exceeded the goals of the campaign without this dedicated group of volunteers.

In other words, I couldn't have done it without people just like you. Just like you, some of these very successful, high-powered individuals were more than a little intimidated by the thought of fundraising. Just like you, they needed some advice and guidance. Just like you, they needed a useful and accessible toolbox for fundraising success from someone who has seen it all.

I was on a plane home sitting next to a man who was minding his own business, reading. Our flight attendant was sufficiently distracted and forgot to give us our all-important water and pretzels. After commiserating over our shared frustration fueled by thirst and hunger, he and I struck up a conversation. As it turned out, he is a very successful executive who has had a year to pursue other ventures (with a non-compete clause from his former employer) while waiting to take a new position. During this time, he and his wife were asked to head up the capital campaign for their children's school, which had been damaged by Hurricane Harvey. They were reluctant, saying, "don't make me fundraise." They wanted to do anything but this to help the school. However, they realized that their many ties in the community could make a significant difference, and they needed to take the bull by the horns. Although this couple is successful in every other realm including their careers, children's development, and personal achievements, they didn't think that they could lead a successful fundraising campaign. Over many months, they tried and failed more than once, they floundered, and they got back up. They learned the hard way, but discovered some simple rules that led, ultimately, to reaching their goals. Now, they are loving every minute of fundraising for such a great cause. They are successful, and they want to do more.

By the time you finish reading this book, I hope you will not only have the confidence to fundraise with the best of them but also love every minute of it as much as I do.

You'll learn that it's easy when you believe in the cause and know that you are making a difference. It's fun when you are successful, whether that's because you have won (which can be rewarding in and of itself) or because you have helped others (also quite rewarding). It definitely feels good when you have the opportunity to surround yourself with wonderful donors. What better way to spend your time than with people smart enough to make a lot of money and nice enough to share it with others? Especially when they share a passion for the same cause!

Before we begin, thank you for being one of those people. Thank you for sharing your time, talents, and resources with your chosen organization to make your community and the world a little better, one fundraiser at a time. Thank you for conveying your passion for the cause with others. I hope this book will help you get out there and sell your cookies. Just remember, whatever happens, there's always a box of Samoas in it for you!

"The journey of a thousand miles starts with a single step."

— Lao Tzu

1
TAKING THE FIRST STEP

YOU KNOW THE FEELING, YOU'VE BEEN THERE. You're there right now. Panic, dread, nausea.

You knew this day was coming from the moment you were asked to join the board. You just didn't think it would come so soon. You thought you'd have more time. You thought you'd be better prepared.

Your mouth goes dry, your palms are sweaty. There's the word, again - fundraiser. "Please," you think, "no, anything, I'll make whatever contribution is necessary! I'll do whatever it takes — sell the house, take the kids out of private school, anything! Just DON'T MAKE ME FUNDRAISE!!!"

Calm down, take a deep breath. You're okay. This little tome is your guide on the road to fundraising acceptance. By the end, you'll not only be all right with this whole fundraising thing, you'll be looking forward to the next one! Just remember, only use your new-found powers for good—a good cause, that is.

CHEAT SHEET FOR HIGHLY EFFECTIVE FUNDRAISING VOLUNTEERS:

- **Be proactive**
Don't wait for a chance encounter or for a staff member to remind you, slowly chip away at all that you need to do.

- **Be creative**
Bring ideas – ones that involve your own sweat equity as well as that of the management team.

- **Think big**
Be emboldened to ask for extraordinary support.

- **Be empathetic**
When speaking with prospective donors, consider their own goals—not just those of the organization.

- **Seek to understand, then be understood**
Learn as much as you can about the organization-including its mission and relevance to society so that you can share this.

- **Sharpen the saw**
Continually research—set aside a little time every week. Use that information to find new ways to express the importance of the organization.

- **Find your voice**
Practice, practice, practice. Get ever better at your engagement of potential donors.

- **No lone-wolf behavior**
Include others in your strategy and in your meetings. It will be more effective if you work with others to take advantage of their knowledge and experience.

- **Have fun**
This can be a labor of love—make it one.

If you are the lead fundraiser, give this list to all your volunteers!

Chances are you've been fundraising already and just didn't realize it. You wouldn't have been asked to donate your time and talents to a board if your passion for the mission weren't already well known within your organization and community. Your friends, family, and colleagues already know about your commitment to the cause, so it will come as no surprise to them when you do finally make the ask. They've been expecting it.

Look back on conversations you've had over the last few months. How often does a discussion of the latest local news story end with you saying, "Oh, my organization is addressing that issue by doing_____ in the community."? When a friend mentions she's trying to get more exercise, how often do you mention that your organization has a walkathon coming up? How many of your social media posts are related to the organization's main cause?

See? If you weren't already a spokesperson for the organization, you wouldn't have been asked to be a volunteer fundraiser in the first place. So, pat yourself on the back and realize the hard part is over — you have enthusiasm and passion for the mission that will convince even the most skeptical potential donor to sit down with you to discuss this specific ask. You're halfway there!

One of my friends who is not a fundraising fan shared: "I realized I have a lot of friends who will give a nominal donation just to support me in something to which I'm committed. I have no hesitation in letting people know what I am supporting. Now, after I let them know what I'm doing, I've started asking them to make a contribution. A fair percentage of them will give $50 (or $100 or $250) just because I was willing to ask. So, if I send my request out to 250 people and get half of them to respond and donate a nominal amount, I've made $10,000 for my organization. It's amazing how it puts me into the upper echelon of a lot of board members because a lot of them don't even try. It isn't hard to ask your friends and just see what happens."

Okay, so there's a little more to it than that. That's what this book is about. It's about getting you through the steps that begin with you learning about the campaign and end with getting the donations you need to fulfill your commitment to the cause. It's about you taking these steps, learning a few lesson, and making them your own. It's about getting you from panic to peace by letting you in on the secrets to a successful fundraising campaign for volunteers and professionals alike.

By the end of this book, you will learn to fundraise so effortlessly and effectively, you will be surprised by how much you enjoy it. You might not be begging for the next opportunity (though, you might), but you'll definitely have the framework and practical advice to make you successful at this sometimes daunting endeavor of asking others for their money.

"No one is useless in this world who lightens the burden of it to anyone else."

—Charles Dickens

2

ASSESSING THE SITUATION

Whose job is this anyway?

You might be wondering, at this point, why they're even asking you to fundraise for them. Isn't this their job? You were just minding your own business at the meeting when out of nowhere, you're expected to ask people for money. Outrageous! Certainly, that's why the CEO or Director of Development is paid. What kind of outfit are they running here?

Well, you're half right. If your organization is lucky enough to have a development department, they do have paid staff that takes on the role of soliciting donations. However, the best administrators avail themselves of all available resources to raise money for an important cause—and you are one of those resources.

Generally, fundraising staff (or a fundraising consultant if there are not staff members) spend their time on the following:

- Frame fundraising goals based on prospective donors and project priorities
- Develop strategies of engagement for all donors
- Handle all the mass solicitations—online, phone, direct mail
- Plan events and tours to engage donors
- Communicate with board members, volunteers, and donors about the organization

According to one national survey, 40% of non-profit CEOs spend 5 to 10 hours per week dealing with board members. Almost 30% spend 11 to 19 hours, and 20% spend 20 hours or more dealing with board members. The best CEOs and executive teams never ask volunteers to do anything that the paid administrators can do. They ask their volunteers to help with the projects and prospects that only they can address. And they have a well-oiled system for their volunteers with timelines and expectations.

WHAT THE PAID STAFF AND/OR CHAIRS HAVE ALREADY DONE BEFORE YOU ARRIVED:

1. Emailed everyone to make sure the date of the meeting worked for everyone.
2. Scheduled and rescheduled the meeting in a long series of emails.
3. Finalized minutes from last meeting.
4. Prepared an agenda for the current meeting.
5. Arranged the room and organized food, drink and staff for current meeting.
6. Reviewed annual budget with eye to programs and

     mission to see where need and shortfalls lay.

7. Developed case statements. (see p. 28 for definition)

8. Decided on best type of fundraiser to meet those challenges or prepare for growth in programs offered to enhance the community.

9. Prepared a gift table. (see p. 33 for definition)

10. Researched other organizations in the area for current fundraising campaigns and event schedules.

11. Decided on named or sponsorship levels.

12. Researched donors.

13. Researched *you*.

14. Assigned donors for solicitation based on best fit with each volunteer.

15. Prepared assets for you to use in your fundraising efforts including solicitation letters, brochures, charts, impact tables, sponsorship documents, matching information, letters of intent/pledge forms, videos, images for social media, thank you cards/gifts, and more (you'll learn about all these quite soon).

16. Created a timeline for the planning phase, quiet phase and public phase.

17. Developed a budget with anticipated expenses to be approved by board.

18. Prepared a list of vendors, etc. needed to accomplish fundraising effort.

19. Devised a schedule/calendar for subsequent planning/progress meetings.

20. And, set aside time for follow-up.

Phew! Aren't you glad you're only in charge of asking a few people to support your cause?

What kind of fundraiser is it?

After the shock wears off, the first thing you'll realize is you missed it when they told you what the fundraiser actually is. Take a look in front of you. See those notes? It's in there somewhere. You're looking for words like event, Fun Run, Capital Campaign, or Annual Fund.

In the course of your tenure on the board or committee, you're likely to come across any and all of these. Once you know the definitions of each, you'll know what to expect and what's expected from you. It's nice to know that no matter the organization or the cause, some things are universal in the land of fundraising. So, let's take a look at the types of fundraising you're likely to encounter and what they mean for you in more detail.

First of all, you should consider any fundraising drive—from a Giving Day to a Gala to an Endowment drive—a "campaign." Language matters. A campaign is about moving to the next level and raising sights. Campaigns are a time when the specific goals of the organization are well articulated, and donors can be asked for a stretch gift. It's the organization's "time in the sun," and, thus, you can be emboldened to ask for extraordinary support. The most successful campaigns are linked to the organization's or institution's long-range strategic plan and a single-minded focus. So, don't be afraid to call your effort a campaign. They work.

Now, back to the question at hand, what kind of campaign is it?

There are two primary kinds of philanthropic gifts: those which take time for the donor to consider (usually called a major gift), and those that are an immediate decision (usually called an annual gift). The former often requires that family members get involved and professional advisors, as well. The latter is typically given on the spot in the form of a check or online donation. If only it ended there! Within these two categories are several subcategories, and you'll have to learn to master them all on your way to fundraising super-stardom.

ANNUAL FUND

Once a year, you are likely asked to contribute to the agency's annual fund. This sort of fundraising can occur throughout the year as the organization keeps trying for that once-per-year or annual gift. However, if you are asked to help support this effort as a volunteer, it is best in a fixed and limited time period, say the last four months of the year when American donors tend to make year-end contributions in preparation for tax-season.

Annual funds are generally focused on raising unrestricted gifts which can be used for programs, payroll, or just generally keeping the agency up and running. Unrestricted and discretionary gifts are the lifeblood of any non-profit and keep the doors open. Throughout the year, these are solicited in any number of ways: direct mail, email, link on the website, monthly pledges, In Memorium gifts, events, social media drives, and, of course, through volunteer fundraising efforts.

Count yourself lucky if this is the sort of fundraising you've just been asked to do. It means you're not involved in a multi-year effort, and you'll probably be off the hook in a few months. However, after the unmitigated success you are about to achieve, be ready and grateful to be asked to participate every year!

CAPITAL CAMPAIGN

Nice work! You're a part of a well-established organization with deep roots in the community. It has a four-star rating on Charity Navigator and most people are aware of its mission. You and your friends save the date every year for the annual gala, and you expect to be asked to just keep doing what you're doing until ... uh oh ... you're asked to play a key role in their upcoming capital campaign. Oh, dear.

A capital campaign is a major, multi-year commitment. In most ways, it is the most rewarding for volunteer fundraisers because at the end, there is a visible reminder of all your efforts—sometimes it is a building, others an endowment. You, and your prospects, can be sure that the funds and the organization will bring lasting, positive change to your community. Also, often it's easier for volunteer fundraisers to have a longer timeline because a prospective donor's "not right now" can easily turn into a "yes" over the course of the campaign. Many times, they will see friends and colleagues supporting your cause and want to jump on the band-wagon. A little success often breeds a lot of success.

A word of warning before we go on: Generally, you should only commit to helping a few of your favorite causes. Depending on your circumstances, you might feel so blessed in your life that you want to spread the wealth to all who ask. In any endeavor, you can't be effective if you're spread too thin. Narrow your focus to one or two causes about which you are really passionate. If you are part of a capital campaign for one of them, make that your primary focus for the length of the campaign. Feel free to keep giving your money to the others, but focus your time and efforts on just the one. The other causes will thank you when their time comes.

TIMELINE FOR CAPITAL CAMPAIGN

The timeline for a campaign is usually over two or more years and should be divided into phases.

• Planning
Let's figure out what is humanly possible to do.

• Quiet
Don't tell the press or public. Keep the hard dollar goal in you mind, not on your website (at this point, nothing about the campaign should be on the site). Keep asking potential donors about their interest in your cause.

• Public
Campaign information is available for all to see. You and the staff are shouting from the rafters, "Hey, everybody, here we are! We think what we are seeking to do is really important."

• Finale

We made it! We can really be of great service to the community for a long time. Take the time to celebrate your success.

EVENT FUNDRAISING (Gala/Party; -A-Thon)

Okay, so you already know all about this one. You've been to countless galas, luncheons, and fashion shows. Once, you even participated in a 5K (once being the operative word). You had fun and felt good about spending your money to support various causes in your community. It's likely you'll be asked at some point to help with this kind of fundraising. Well, hang onto your hat, you're about to find out how much time and work actually goes into pulling off this "one day" of fundraising.

This most common type of fundraiser really should be a subset of the other types. These days, an event is typically tied to any one of the other sorts of fundraising. A luncheon or gala is generally an annual event to keep donors giving every year. If you're involved in a capital campaign, there might be several associated events. For example, if the campaign is to raise funds for a new building, there might be a kick-off party for the campaign, a groundbreaking event, and a gala to celebrate once the building is finished.

The timeline for planning a gala or fundraising party usually starts six months out and involves an extensive list of to-do items. This is a category where you are planning for the worst and hoping for the best. Be ready if all hell breaks loose! Staying organized and keeping an eye on your checklist should help.

Event Checklist

- ☐ Objectives of event identified
- ☐ Select all necessary event chairs (Gift Committee, Host Committee, Auction, PR, etc.)
- ☐ Secure the venue/date (for some organizations, the date is set in stone and venue is flexible; for others, the venue is the more important element)
- ☐ Food/drink - caterer hired if not included at the venue
- ☐ Decide on entertainment and decor
- ☐ Hire florist if venue doesn't provide one
- ☐ Hire graphic designer for invitations, program, signage, awards, etc. (and printer if necessary)
- ☐ Send "Save the Date" three months ahead of event
- ☐ Decide on need for video program and hire videographer
- ☐ Hire photographer
- ☐ Acquire auction items to be donated
- ☐ Secure sponsorships
- ☐ Send invitations six weeks ahead
- ☐ Order awards if appropriate
- ☐ Invite press with pre-event release
- ☐ Set program - timeline and speakers (send to print)
- ☐ RSVPs collected
- ☐ Print name tags and place cards
- ☐ Dry-run of program
- ☐ Purchase thank you gift for host
- ☐ Send post-event press release

EMERGENCY FUNDING

This is exactly what it sounds like. Typically, you won't be involved in a big way because the timeline for the fundraising is so short. There's really not enough time to delegate this sort of fundraising to volunteers. You'll likely just be asked to donate and spread the word. Ask people when enthusiasm and emotions run high and they will understand the immediate impact.

In the aftermath of most major storms from hurricanes to fires, many local organizations have to scramble to get services in place and ask for timely donations. As a volunteer, you should insist and help your organization have a plan in place to deploy asks and to receive money before the emergency occurs. You and the staff should be ready to man the phones to get the word out, have an online portal to accept donations, and have an email and social media strategy in place for when the electricity comes back on. With a plan in place, it's possible for you and your fellow board members to be a meaningful part of the solution when the time comes.

There are times when a cause hits a community and overtakes everyone's heart. For Houston, that was Hurricane Harvey. Volunteers came out of the woodwork, funds came from every corner of the country. That disaster was profound, but I was in awe of how quickly people worked side by side, worked cooperatively, and worked toward helping others. From the tragedy came a good reminder—people are fundamentally good and want to help their fellow citizens.

"A goal without a plan is just a wish."
—Antoine de Saint-Exupéry

3

PLANNING FOR SUCCESS

THOUGH THERE ARE SEVERAL TYPES OF CAMPAIGNS, all campaigns follow a broad model which has been proven successful over the years. Crucial is the creation of a committee of anywhere from three to 40+ volunteers. It must be led by a Chair or Co-Chairs, who are typically the most generous or most visible donors to the organization. If this is you, you're probably using this book as a training tool for the less experienced fundraisers amongst you. If this is not you, it will be soon!

Some projects are big, some are small (at least in amount to be raised). I was a swim team mom, and of course happy to jump in as a volunteer to raise funds and sell baked goods for the summer swim team meets. When you jump in as a volunteer, you become chair of the effort pretty quickly. If that happens to you, embrace it. It's sometimes better to be in control of the situation and follow your instincts. You can get there as fast as you want.

For this committee to work effectively, you'll need to know who does what, when and why. Four simple tools can help you get through the planning stages and set you off on the path to success: the Ghostbuster List, Meeting Agendas, Case Statements, and Gift Tables.

GHOSTBUSTER LIST

If your organization has staff who fundraise, make sure all are clear on who is doing what. You will never have fun or be tremendously successful if those roles are confused or you are duplicating efforts. See it as a partnership. As a volunteer, you are giving your brand, your contacts, and your time. Every person plays an important role, but you do play different roles.

Your chairpersons will work closely with the staff to define those roles for the specific campaign. Working together, they will provide you with a clear timeline, a clear path to success, a clear message that your time as a volunteer fundraiser is valued, and a clear organizational chart of who does what.

My staff kid me because I call the "who does what" the Ghostbuster List. As in the line from the movie(s), "Who ya gonna call?" The answer in the movie is "Ghostbusters"...Your answers need to be:

Ghostbuster List
I will call/email _____...
- ☐ if I have a check for deposit.
- ☐ if I need more copies of the materials/pledge forms.
- ☐ if I need help navigating or adding to the website.
- ☐ if I need someone to go on a call with me.
- ☐ if I need to find out how we are doing.

MEETINGS AND AGENDAS

Feel free to skip this section if you're not chairing the campaign. However, when you do take charge, you'll find the first step to success is a well-planned planning meeting. Yes, you heard me, you have to plan for planning. Poorly planned meetings are one of the biggest hindrances to keeping a volunteer force motivated and successful.

No matter the type of campaign you are heading, you will have several meetings with the entire board (and sometimes staff) to plan the campaign and monitor progress along the way. Generally, the first meeting will determine the type of campaign, how the board members can help individually, and map out a timeline of future meetings that work for everyone. Subsequent meeting will focus on overall progress, ways to improve, and gratitude for the progress already achieved. No matter how many meetings your campaign might need, everyone benefits when they are well-planned and well-organized.

SAMPLE VOLUNTEER FUNDRAISING BOARD MEETING

Meeting #1 Agenda
- Welcome from the Chair(s)
- Introductions and "Why I Joined" from all committee members
- Charge to board
- Timeline for board
- Tasks for board
- Tasks for individual members
- Set fundraising goals

Note to the meeting organizer(s):
Before the meeting, give participants the agenda and draft committee charge (and nothing else)
- Remember: The more paper, the less discussion
- Ask all to bring a calendar or phone so the next three meetings can be scheduled
- Bring a list of any black-out and important dates, including anything big happening in the city, cultural holidays, or other deadlines within the organization itself
- Have a list of tasks you would like the committee to address
- Let others talk

You can give the committee volunteers note or doodle pads with "Why I joined the _____ campaign" printed on it.
Alternately, you can give them a preprinted placemat

sized sheet telling them precisely how they should solicit:

Name	Contact Info	Objective of correspondence	Follow-up	Thank you note (Y)
What Have I Learned?				
My Goal:				
What do I believe I need to succeed?				

Two weeks before Meeting #2
Chair should
- Call each member to stress importance of participation
- Ask each member what s/he has done since last meeting and to be ready to report on that
- Be prepared to give a committee member a small or large something to do before the meeting, if they have done nothing so far

Meeting #2 Sample Agenda
- Welcome
- Review of Organization Benchmarks and YTD progress
- Updates by each member
- Analytics update
  o How do we compare with other similar

organizations?
- o Are we raising more?
- o Are we spending less?
- o Are we missing opportunities?
- o How can we get better?
- o Does volunteer structure work for you? For the organization?
- o Do we have the right size volunteer base?

Meeting #3
- Welcome
- Review of Organization Benchmarks and Year to date progress
- Updates by each member
- Messaging
  - o Who knows what we do?
  - o What are we hearing outside in the community as we talk with donors?
  - o How specifically can we expand our reach?

Tangible benefits to volunteers matter—things like mugs, t-shirts, pins, hats—it's more the symbolic value than the actual value of the merchandise.
Go to Etsy and get something fun made that you can share with your fellow volunteers to celebrate their victories along the way. You can also consider doing the same for donors at various levels, you might even be pleasantly surprised at what comes back to you.

Sometimes it doesn't take much to make a big difference. I know of one board volunteer at Penn State who was at his country club in Florida for the winter and noticed someone he didn't know wearing a Penn State cap. He walked up and started a conversation. Turned out, the fellow was a big fan but had never given. So, our volunteer picked up the phone, called the Vice President for Development and made the connection. Within nine months, the fellow wearing the cap had given $500,000 to Penn State. Thanks to the lucky combination of branded swag and a great volunteer who always had the university on his mind, we scored big.

CASE STATEMENTS
YOUR CASE FOR SUPPORT

Again, if you're not one of the head honchos, this section probably isn't for you. You *will* be getting one of these statements eventually, but you won't be preparing it yourself. You can read just enough to figure out what it is and skip all of the how to get there.

So, for those of you in the position of having to prepare these documents, you might have a couple of supplementary meetings in which you will have to delve into the nitty-gritty of the campaign. You should be able to answer four questions to bring your campaign into focus:

1. Why is our mission important?
2. Why now?
3. What can we accomplish?
4. What will it take?

Keep it simple: Do you need to meet the budget requirements for next year? Raise money for a new building? Start an endowment? Plug a deficit? I won't lie to you, that last one is quite difficult. You have to address honestly and clearly the situation that has led you to that spot. Why should anyone rescue you? There *can* be good reasons: maybe a hurricane wiped out all your homeless shelters, or the needs for the organization outweighed its capacity last year. All the others are easy.

Then, write your statement about why someone might want to make a gift, called in the business "A Case for Support" or "Case Statement." Keep it short. Make sure that you can say it in one sentence, only add more to underscore and provide context. But it's your first sentence that will grab someone or not.

A good friend is part of a billionaire family. Any organization where he serves on the board and gives, his family could satisfy the whole campaign goal. However, that wouldn't be the point. He's a savvy volunteer who knows that our real non-profit goals are only reached with a broader group of support. So, to make things happen, he gives his more precious resource—time. And he does make them happen. Any organization to which he lends his heart and time moves toward being the best in the nation. I asked him what was the best advice he would give another volunteer fundraiser. He said: "Remember that money follows ideas. You aren't just asking for money, you are asking for support for an idea that will change the world, make it a better world. Whether that's for a neighborhood, city, or the country. So make sure that you have a good idea in mind before you launch."

Always remember that virtually no one gives to a sinking ship. You need to live in the space between "need" and "a positive difference." Perhaps the best way to explain is by way of examples.

EXAMPLES OF CASE STATEMENTS FOR AN ANNUAL FUND

What Your Gift Can Do: The Impact of a Current Gift to Our School
We are seeking $200,000 to provide operating funds for next year. The cause is strong, and donor dollars make the difference between doing good work and great work.
Securing gifts for current use discretionary spending is one of the highest fundraising priorities for us. These gifts provide the essential resources to meet new needs and seize opportunities as they arise. Gifts of all sizes matter. Individual discretionary gifts have impact, see examples below:
$10   Purchase school lunch for a week
$25   Buy a flask for the chemistry lab
$50   Purchase books for each child in one classroom
$100   Buy a school uniform for a scholarship student
$300   Buy a stand-alone printer

What Your Gift Can Do: The Impact of an Unrestricted Gift

We are seeking funds so the organization can do its work well. Your donation allows our organization to reach its goals and serve its constituents while not worrying about running out of money during the year. In the most recent years, our Annual Fund has consistently accounted for approximately 60% of the annual budget. The fund is used for general costs and a significant portion is allocated to program funding. While our organization has a wonderful local reputation, the notion that it is "rich" and doesn't need annual support simply isn't true. The case for yearly support becomes even more evident when other factors are considered:

- Student tuition only covers about 60% of the costs of educating the student.
- Scholarships help us to recruit a stronger and more diverse group of students, helping those who want a great education.

EXAMPLES OF CASE STATEMENTS FOR A CAPITAL CAMPAIGN

What Your Gift Can Do: The Impact of a Gift for a new Building or Renovation

We are seeking funds to build and furnish a new wing for our Food Bank. The community's need has gone from 5,000 meals per day to 10,000 meals per day as a result of growing homelessness.

(add one page of facts about the campaign to make the ask more concrete)

What the new facility will do:
- Embrace and anticipate new technology
- Improve acoustics and lighting in teaching areas
- Provide study spaces
- Update and improve furnishings
- Encourage informal communication and meetings between faculty and students, students and students
- Number of square feet to be added:
- Number of renovated square feet:
- Total cost

What Your Gift Can Do: The Impact of Starting a Permanent Fund

We are seeking to start a permanent endowment, funds that will assure the longevity and strength of our organization. We are asking those who believe in supporting us each year to make a gift that will keep on giving long after each of us is gone. We will only spend the income from the fund each year, leaving intact the principal to spend over the years.

SET THE GIFT TABLE
A Map To Millions

No, it's not the fun kind at a wedding or birthday party, but it can lead to major gifts. Unless you are a gift chair or the agency's CEO, you won't be the one with the tedious task of looking over charts, calculating payments and distribution, and crunching the numbers to put it all together. However, you will need to know how success happens and how you can play a part.

Remember, up to this point, the staff and chairs have already determined the dollar amount necessary and, consequently, what kind of campaign is required to fulfill that need. They looked at their current donor pool, analyzed the kinds of gifts they received in the past, and projected the amount they could expect in stretch gifts. They researched other non-profits in the area to compare the scope of their project with that of other institutions which were successful in asking for similar funds, and noted some of their major donors. They paired their past major donors with new prospects based on demographic data such as geography, age, type of work, political affiliation, or alma mater.

Then, and only then, do they sit down to construct a gift table.

So, what is it? It is a chart or road map to let you know how many gifts of what size you will need to make your goal. And, done right, also tells you how many people you will need to ask at each level in order to make your goal.

Roughly speaking, about one third of your goal will come from the top 10 donors; a third from the next 100 donors; and the remaining third will come from all other donors.

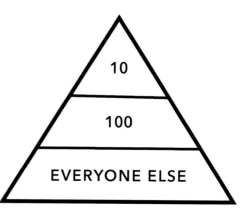

Don't be fooled, using a gift table isn't as simple as collecting $50,000 donations from 20 major gifts prospects if your campaign goal is $1,000,000 — or even 10,000 gifts of $100. It's really a pyramid with a few, but largest, gifts at the top. Generally, an organization aims for the lead gift to be about 20% of the fundraising goal. One thing to remember before you start your gift table is that you have a stated dollar goal, whatever the size, to help fulfill the mission of the campaign. You believe in the project, but that doesn't mean every philanthropist will be interested. It certainly doesn't mean that every rich person will be interested. Your organization has a specific mission and role, so think about the people who are passionate about that mission. Built into the gift table is the expectation that you will need to speak with and ask multiple people to get one "yes."

THE GIFT PYRAMID

SET UP A GIFT PYRAMID

RAISE $100,000

15,000 Donors in Database

- **3% Participation**
- **450 Donors**

1 Donor at $10,000 = $10,000	
4 Donors at $4,000 = $16,000	
5 Donors at $1,600 = $8,000	
40 Donors at $500 = $20,000	
60 Donors at $200 = $12,000	
340 Donors at $100 = $34,000	

Gift tables can be tough but it isn't like a Pythagorean Theorem. (In case you have forgotten from high school math, that's the square of the hypotenuse of a right triangle is equal to the sum of the square of the other two sides.) Maybe it is easier to think of it as an Excel spreadsheet where you can feed in numbers that fit your circumstances. A gift table can, indeed, be just that, a spreadsheet that answers a few questions about the campaign.

Questions that you want to answer with your gift table:

- How many gifts do we need at what level to get to our goal?

- Do we need a whopper naming gift? If so, what seems right? (Ideally, it will be 30-50% of your goal.)

- How many mid-level gifts do we need? Is it 20? If so, we likely need 60 people we can ask at that level.

What about the lower-level gifts? Do we need 100?

Those will be easier to come by than the mid-level gifts. You might need to ask about 200 people. You should never assume that all lights will be green in this process. It's better to be prepared for the "no" and be pleasantly surprised by the "yes."

- What is realistic in terms of getting a few big gifts to make the project easier to fund?
- How many do we expect to ask to get one gift?

Goal	Number of People to Ask	Number of Gifts Needed
Biggest Gift	5	1
Mid-Sized Gifts	15	5
Smallest Gifts	30	10

If you are including private foundations in your gift table, then expect to have to put a proposal or application in writing. And know that increasingly foundations are looking for collaborations between organizations. With the explosion of non-profits in the last twenty years, every foundation is inundated with proposals. The non-profits working with other non-profits, squeezing efficiency at every turn, and getting the community to talk to each other will likely be the winners.

Do some research along the way. Who is giving to the campaign thus far? Are they from a particular neighborhood? From a certain generation? Are they past donors who have just stepped up to make a bigger gift during the campaign? Are they long lost donors you brought back into the fold?

With a multi-year campaign, it is important that you build the gift table and prioritize from the top ones down.

The chairs or staff will provide you with this overall gift table for the entire campaign, but you should also make your own gift table to track your personal efforts in the campaign. Perhaps it's helpful to think of the overall chart as the gift pyramid, while your efforts can be mapped using a simple gift chart like the one below.

Gift Amount	Number of Gifts Needed	Number of Prospects	Total	Number of Prospects for My Goal
$20,000	1	5	$20,000	N/A
$10,000	1	3	$10,000	N/A
$5,000	2	8	$10,000	1 long shot
$1,000	8	20	$8,000	5 to get 1
$500	20	60	$10,000	10 to get 3
$100	250	675	$25,000	25 to get 14
$50 and below	350	500	$17,000	40 to get 22
			Total to raise: $100,000	My Goal $5,000

The campaign gift table is to raise your sights and see what's possible. Your personal gift table is a tool to keep you focused and motivated. It's your own personal tracking thermometer that you should be excited to fill in and check off your progress!

AS THE TIMELINE PROGRESSES

So, you've made it through the first meeting. You have a clear idea of the campaign type and objective. You've been given materials to distribute, names and addresses, a timeline, stats and scripts, a gift table, and Ghostbusters List. You're aware that your most important responsibility is to promote the cause and solicit potential donors. You know what's expected of you and what's beyond your purview. You've even reading this book to help you through the anxiety of fundraising and become wildly successful at the endeavor.

But, wait, there's more!

As you can see on your timeline, there are several upcoming meetings regarding the campaign and your involvement. In preparation for these meetings, one of the chairs or someone on staff will contact you for an update on your progress. Be prepared for questions such as: How are you doing with your efforts? Where are you in your list? What challenges have you faced? What can we do to help?

In subsequent meetings, the person in charge of the campaign will combine the answers from all the volunteers involved with the campaign and make sure you're the first to hear how the campaign is progressing, changes in staff and board, challenges, and any adjustments to the campaign to address those potential difficulties. You'll be given updated documents, recognition, a gift or two to mark your achievements (if you're on one of the best kind of boards, which I'm sure you are), a new fact sheet with the updated stats and script, and more words of encouragement.

Somewhere along the way, you'll learn that success comes not only from meeting the dollar goal but also from enhancing the visibility of the organization, getting more people enthusiastic about the mission, and serving more members of the community. You and the board should stop every once and awhile to recognize the progress you've made and celebrate every one of those successes. When you do, the fundraising process becomes a joyful process instead of a bleak obligation.

My daughter was volunteer co-chair of her Yale reunion fund recently, and I asked her why she was willing to take on the responsibility given her hectic schedule. Initially, she said she was "guilted into it." After a minute of reflection, she realized she just wanted to give back to an organization which had done something important for her and give future students the same shot at success. She and her fellow co-chair got the kind of support from the staff outlined in this book—including scripts, a gift table, and names with contact information—and they made their goal!

"We make a living by what we get; we make a life by what we give."
—Winston Churchill

4

YOU FIRST

FUNDRAISING SUCCESS IS ABOUT BELIEVING IN THE cause. How do you show others you believe in the cause? You put your own hard-earned money where your mouth is and you give. It doesn't have to be one of the top tiers of your gift table, but it has to be of some significance, especially as it relates to your financial capacity. Don't give until it hurts, give until it feels good.

By all means, be one of the first to pledge. Again, it doesn't have to be the biggest, but it should be right for you and your level of commitment. Don't wait to be asked. Talk to the organization's CEO or campaign chair about your gift intentions and how you can make an impact. Then, you can cross yourself off the list and put a check mark on the gift table. You'll be a hero on the board, and you won't have another thing on your pesky to-do list.

In all seriousness, being the first to give allows you to see all the steps in the process before asking someone else to donate. If it's an event, check out the process of purchasing tickets online. See if the process is smooth or if there are technical issues that need to be fixed. If it's a major gift, find out how many people you need to speak to before you can decide on a number. You can ascertain if your financial advisor thinks it's more beneficial in the current economy to give the donation in a lump sum or pledge it over a number of years. You can answer any objections by family members before you have to answer them from your list of potential donors. No matter the size or kind of donation, when you donate first, you get practice.

Not only does being first give you hands-on experience with the process, but it will also have a significant impact on your ability to convince others to donate. One of the first questions you will get is, "How much did you give?" If you haven't made a gift but are asking others to do so, they will wonder why they should commit if you haven't. You'd think something was a little fishy with that, too, right?

"My friend...care for your psyche... know thyself, for once we know ourselves, we may learn how to care for ourselves."

—Socrates

5

KNOW THYSELF, THY CAUSE, AND THY PROSPECT

YOU KNOW IF YOU LIKE TO PLAY TENNIS OR YOU would rather watch tennis on TV. You know if you like mystery books or poetry. You know if you would rather travel or stay home. You know that you are not the type to enjoy fundraising. What? How can you know if you haven't even tried yet?

You've proven time and again that you can do anything to which you put your mind. You rise to every challenge. That's part of who you are. Don't dismiss it.

No matter what type of person you are, fundraising allows you to learn more about yourself. You can see this as a time to learn a new skill that will have utility in other areas, as well. For one thing, fundraising teaches you to listen. It helps you to forge new connections with interesting and generous people. It forces you to convey a positive attitude as you think about the good your organization is doing. You will learn humility and understand your own comfort zones. Fundraisers typically do not claim the limelight — that is for the donors. (After all, the donors gave the money!)

Fundraising will help you see your place in the world differently as you act as an advocate for those your organization helps. You're not just asking people to donate money for a building, you're asking them to help provide shelter so abused women can find a second chance at life or underprivileged students have a place to learn or families of cancer patients a place to live during treatment. You will start to see your part in the larger whole and understand yourself a little more each time you make the ask.

My husband is a great salesman. (And he's a great husband—often accompanying me on donor trips, donor calls, and goodness knows endless dinners and galas.) In fact, he's a much better salesman than almost anyone, he asks for the order and always wants to go for more.

While I admire that quality greatly, I know myself. That kind of salesmanship isn't what I do best. I am best at listening and interpreting what prospective donors want to do, then translating that into how it fits with everyone's goals and interests. While we have very different styles, we get to the same place. Just as I have to know myself and my strengths to be effective, you need to know your voice, your style, and embrace it. Be authentic.

KNOW THY CAUSE

Easy, right? Of course you know the cause. We established this at the very beginning. You've been advocating for this organization all over the place. The mission is tattooed on your forehead. Every social media post is related to your cause. You've got this!

Well, not so fast. You've made a great start, and you certainly won't falter when asked about the organization generally. However, this is the part where you have to get into specifics.

Look over the materials you've been given to support the campaign. That's where you'll find them. You might not have a document labeled "Case for Support," but the guts are in your head or in something you have read. I'm willing to bet it's in the body of a letter or website you've been given. It might be on page two of a brochure, but you'll find it if you look for words like, "Your donation supports X meals for Y students," or "X facility will allow us to house Y% more women and children per year."

Whatever the case for support, the key is to determine what points will resonate with your prospects. Generally, what resonates are visions that are results oriented and about people helping people. Money follows ideas.

Again, make sure the case is specific and not just about the organization's mission as a whole. Even if you are soliciting for the annual fund, tailor your presentation to discuss why private gifts make a difference. (Of course, if your organization is supported 100% by donations, then you don't need to do more than state that the organization shuts its doors without private giving.) You will need information about *where* gifts were allocated in the past—if used for an unrestricted fund or director's fund—and *how* that money has been spent the last few years. If it went for meals for students or landscaping or books, you can use that granularity to convince donors to give.

Make sure to write everything down and create a script that you can use as a jumping-off point for discussions. You'll want to couch the hard stats in humanitarian terms. Always bring it back to how you are helping actual individuals in your community.

The best volunteers are those who always have the cause somewhere on top of mind. They find ways to talk with their friends, families, and colleagues about the cause. Not always, maybe not even the majority of the time, with an expectation of an ask. But they are still practicing their script, learning from the conversations, and getting themselves more excited about what they are doing. Good things come from every such encounter.

Finally, look at your organization's website. If you are making a claim, make sure it is consistent with whatever is on the website. Guaranteed, someone will follow up with a look after you are gone. It could be the person with whom you met, their financial advisor, or their children who want to make sure that their parents are still making good decisions. If the website is inconsistent with your message and the supporting documents you've been given, you're going to lose the donation. So, check, double check, and tell someone on staff to change the offending materials. They'll thank you later!

KNOW THY PROSPECT

There's a scene at the beginning of Charles Dickens' *A Christmas Carol* that's included in most versions of the film, but few of us really notice. Dickens paints a picture of Scrooge's character by introducing two solicitors using the season to try to drum up donations for those less fortunate.

> They were portly gentlemen, pleasant to behold, and now stood, with their hats off, in Scrooge's office. They had books and papers in their hands, and bowed to him.
> "Scrooge and Marley's, I believe," said one of the gentlemen, referring to his list. "Have I the pleasure of addressing Mr. Scrooge, or Mr. Marley?"
> "Mr. Marley has been dead these seven years," Scrooge replied. "He died seven years ago, this very night."
> "We have no doubt his liberality is well represented by his surviving partner," said the gentleman, presenting his credentials.[1]

Let these nameless gentlemen serve as a cautionary tale for you. It's not just that they were barking up the wrong tree (of course, they were), it's that they didn't even know which tree they were addressing. Presumably, they had a ledger noting that Marley had made a generous donation in the past. However, they were so busy anticipating the

---

[1] Dickens, Charles. (2004). *A Christmas Carol* [Online], Salt Lake City: Project Gutenberg. Available at https://www.gutenberg.org/files/46/46-h/46-h.htm [Accessed November 2019].

money they would receive, they had no idea that Marley had died many years ago or that his partner was a bah-humbug of a prospect.

Of course, these Victorian gentlemen didn't have Google to fall back on. You, on the other hand, have no excuse.

As already mentioned, your list was carefully generated by you or the organization based on certain shared demographics. If your organization hasn't shared the specifics, pick up the phone and ask. A simple, "I'm preparing for my meeting with X, and was hoping you could give me a little background," will likely get you all the information you could want and more. If not, a quick internet search is in your future.

In addition to general information about what the prospect does, what they look like, how they prefer to be addressed, there are specific questions you need to answer such as: Is there any recent history or interaction with the organization of which you should be aware? Find out if there is something in the prospective donor's past connecting them to your organization. For example, if you are raising money for a memory center at a hospital, see if your prospect knows someone with Alzheimer's.

Who else at the organization do they know? Ask if you can contact that person before your visit. (This might be staff or another volunteer. You might say, "I am going to see Suzy, and wonder if there is anything I should know about her, when you last talked to her, etc. And may I mention that we have talked about her generosity and importance to the organization?") And, if you can, know how long it has been since the last interaction with the organization. If it was yesterday, you are in luck. If it was two years ago, you have a bigger challenge but not an impossible one.

All of this information allows you to walk into the meeting knowing what your ask will be. If a prospect has family member with cancer, they will likely be willing to donate much more to fund a cure than to your child's school. That said, there are certainly times when you want to say "give whatever you can," but you will always want to have a specific ask in mind. When you can be specific, it helps the prospective donor know what is an appropriate and significant gift. They may not agree, but at least you're giving them a framework for making a decision. Of course, you can modify your ask during the conversation, but you should have a knowledge-based plan when you walk in the door.

In my years of fundraising billions of dollars, you would think I would be focusing on those who have the biggest yachts and biggest homes. However, I have found it's often those who display their wealth prominently who are in the "acquisition phase" or "enjoying their money phase." Later in life, they may very well want to be philanthropic, but it isn't right for them now. I have found that many who live modestly will give hundreds of thousands or millions to organizations. Their giving brings them much more joy than an extravagant lifestyle. Different strokes for different folks. Moral of the story, don't judge a prospect by his cover.

"I've learned that you shouldn't go through life with a catcher's mitt on both hands, you need to be able to throw something back."

—Maya Angelou

6
PRACTICE MAKES PERFECT

You're well ahead of the game at this point. You're an advocate for the organization, you've accepted the challenge of being a part of this campaign, and you've been your first donor. You practiced the steps your prospects will have to take when they make their donations. You're familiar with the materials you've been given and know the case for support backwards and forwards. You've written out a script and elevator speech with all the pertinent facts. You have a passion for the mission and know the funds are going to further help your community. Everything is falling into place.

Except...

There's still that except. Except you can't see yourself actually asking anyone for money no matter how good the cause. Except you weren't raised that way. Except you're terrified of failing such a worthy cause. Except...

The way you'll be able to stop with the excepts and

realize that you and the cause you represent are exceptional is through practice. Practice is how you've gotten better at everything else you've tried — tennis, piano, driving, typing on a keyboard, learning how to use a new piece of software. Practice is what makes difficult things easier or easy things second nature. Practice might not make perfect, but it does make habit, muscle memory, and the ability to foresee and forestall challenges.

So, practice your script in the mirror every morning when you wake up and at night before you go to bed. Practice over lunch with your best friend or mother, who will undoubtedly give you advice on how to improve. Practice with your significant other every night over dinner until they can recite it for you. Practice the "except" away. Practice, practice, practice.

Many under 40 have never heard of Lee Iacocca, but he was an American hero, the best known corporate CEO for decades. He single-handedly sold America on Chrysler when it was at death's door. He was considered by many to be the consummate salesman, who then went on to chair the Statue of Liberty/Ellis Island national campaign. Iacocca recounted in his autobiography that as a young sales rep, he wrote down his pitch and practiced it over and over again before making his cold calls.

He writes, "Once I had mastered the facts, I worked on how to present them. ... Learning the skills of salesmanship takes time and effort. You have to practice them over and over again until they become second nature."[2]

[2] Iacocca, Lee. (2007). *Iacocca: An Autobiography* [E-book], New York: Bantam Dell.

"Sometimes the bravest and most important thing you can do is show up."
—Brené Brown

7

PUSH YOURSELF
OUT THE DOOR

IF AFTER ALL THAT PRACTICE YOU ARE STILL reluctant, figure out what you can do to just start. Starting doesn't mean rushing headlong into the ask. Starting means making a plan and making an appointment. (If you're raring to go, just skip ahead a couple of pages to *Planners Gonna Plan*, you're all good!)

Let's take this one step at a time. First, take out your calendar. Mark the end of the campaign. If it's an event, you might want to mark the end of the campaign as the print deadline for the program so your prospects can be recognized. If it's a capital campaign, the end date is more fluid and can be two or more years out.

That was easy, right? This next part is going to be a little more difficult. You're going to have to find a few upcoming dates in your busy schedule that work for you to have afternoon or evening meetings. Now that you're looking at your busy schedule, you're going to start thinking about your prospects' busy schedules. Take a deep breath. Don't let that twinge of anxiety turn into a full-blown panic attack. Just pick dates that work for you.

Pick up the phone. Don't worry, you're not calling a single prospect, yet. You're calling the organization. Call the number of the person on your Ghostbuster List who can support you by joining you at meetings. Often times, this will be the CEO or Director of Development. Pick the person with whom you feel the most comfortable and coordinate dates with them. Let them know you'd like to have an informal gathering with some staff and some of the prospects on your list. Yup, that's right, you're having a party.

As a reluctant fundraiser, sometimes the easiest way to start is by surrounding yourself with others who are enthusiastic about the mission and the cause. Those people can lay the groundwork for you and spread their often infectious excitement about the project. You can listen to them and compare their script to yours. You can watch how they interact with potential donors. If they are good (which, of course, they are), note that most of the time, they are engaged in listening to the prospect, not rambling on about the organization.

At your informal gathering, you not only get to surround yourself with these fellow advocates, you get to better know those on your prospect list before you ask them for a one-on-one meeting. Ideally, they will be so enchanted with you and the organization that they make a major gift on the spot. Realistically, you will be able to feel them out and better gauge how to proceed with the next steps and plan accordingly.

Excerpt from a letter I recently received:

I have learned to do things that I enjoy and make the ask a seemingly secondary objective. So, as it turns out, I like having live music concerts at my house. If I invite 100 people, 50 of them will come. Then 50 people will come through other friends or the musicians themselves, and we can raise some money.

Musicians have such a hard time making any kind of money these days that they love doing house concerts. If I offer them whatever comes in from asking for $20 from everyone who attends, they are ecstatic. If they can make $800 to $2000 in one night, they are very happy.

When I put a separate donations basket by the door and ask everybody to contribute to a charity, people usually do it. Last year, after the California wildfires, we raised $1000 apiece for two separate fire fighting or reconstruction organizations at an event that most people thought was just a party. My point is just that if you do something that your friends want to do anyway, it's pretty easy to raise some money on the side. Not a lot, but some.

Then, of course, once someone has donated for a first time, you never know whether they could be persuaded to get more directly involved and give more.

Planners Gonna Plan

Now that you know your prospects a little better and have seen the experts in action, how do you feel? A little more confident? A little more prepared? You should! That was a huge win. No matter how it turns out on an individual basis, you've introduced at least a few new people to your cause. It's even possible you made a few new friends not only for the non-profit but also for yourself in the bargain. Take a minute and pat yourself on the back.

Okay, that's enough. Back to work. You have more planning to do.

Go back to your calendar and pick a few more dates. This time, you're picking the dates that you will commit to calling or emailing prospects. Just schedule a time for one or two calls on each of those days. The worst thing you can do at this point is overdo it and rush the process. Take your time, practice, hone your skills as you go along.

Before you make a single call, plan your list.

Look at the list of prospective donors you were given. Mark the ones who you know best and think are likely to give something just because it's you. These are the ones you'll call first. You have to plan for some early wins to keep your confidence and enthusiasm high. The others on your list may end up surprising you, but make sure you start with a few guaranteed slam dunks.

At this point, you can mark your list in batches of which prospects you plan to call or email first, second, third, etc., but it's not necessary. It's completely up to you and your personality type. Just remember, you're only calling the first batch of prospects over the next few days and only to set up appointments to meet. No big deal.

Wait, I see you picking up that phone. Not so fast. Have you gone back to your calendar to identify the best dates and times for the meeting? Nothing is worse than going back and forth a thousand times on a call or email because dates are scarce. Do you know where you will meet? It really shouldn't be in a noisy restaurant or public area if you're asking for money. Find a place where your prospect will feel comfortable, their home turf, so they don't feel pressured. Have you practiced what you will say on the call to set the meeting? You don't want to stumble straight out of the gate.

Since these first calls are people you know fairly well, all of this will be easier. You probably have a vague idea of their schedules and feel comfortable having them to your home. However, don't just invite them over. You may lose a friend or acquaintance if they think they are just coming over for drinks and all of a sudden you jump into asking them for a donation. Think how you would feel! Make sure they know the purpose of this meeting is to discuss how they might help your organization. Let them know that even if this isn't the right time or cause for them, they are one of the first people you are contacting, and you'd be honored for them to help you practice the ask. No pressure on them, they are helping you refine your skills. Of course, this last tactic is only appropriate if you already have that kind of relationship. Please don't try it with someone you just met at a cocktail party!

Speaking of casual acquaintances, for those on your list you don't already know, start with an email to introduce yourself, the cause, how you acquired their contact info, and that you would like to schedule a time for a call or meeting. Some people prefer communicating this way, some will ignore it, some won't even receive it. However, if you don't know the person, chances are it will be appreciated.

In Nashville, I was on the board of All About Women. I was in awe of what they had started before I arrived—an annual, several-day event which led thousands and thousands of women to healthier lives. It was creative, interactive, and hugely successful. That board needed lots of corporate sponsors, and I was reminded of how hard it is for volunteers to navigate the world of corporate philanthropy. What are the rules? How much lead time does it take? What amount should we request? Do we use our connection to the CEO or go to the person who is in charge of community support? But they jumped in, navigated their connections, and gained the respect of their corporate donors.

SAMPLE PHONE AND EMAIL SCRIPTS

Sample call to someone you know well:

Hi, _____! It was so great to see you at _____. I hope _____ is doing better. (You get it. Start with a little small talk because you're not a rude person.)

Listen, I was hoping we could get together at my place a week from Tuesday (be fairly specific about the place and date) to discuss the campaign I'm working on with _____. I'd love to get you involved at whatever level you feel comfortable. (If this is one of those people with whom you can practice, add that part in, too.) If you're not interested, I totally understand, but I'd really love your feedback on how I came across with my ask for support. Do you have the time to help me out?

Sample call to someone you know a little:

Hi, _____! It was so great to see you at _____. I hope _____ is doing better. (Again, start with a little small talk to establish your past relationship.)

Listen, I was hoping we could get together at _____ a week from Tuesday (be fairly specific about the place and date) to discuss the campaign I'm working on with _____. I'd love to get you involved at whatever level you feel comfortable and get your feedback on the campaign. If that day doesn't work, when is best for you?

Sample call to someone you don't know at all:

Hi, _____, my name is _____ and I was given your number by_____ to discuss the upcoming campaign we're working on. (If you don't know the person, it's best to jump right in. At this point, you should remind them of their connection to the institution you're representing.) The president thought we would be a good fit since you graduated just a few years after me.

I don't know if you received my email that I sent last week, but I was hoping we could get together at your office (remember, offer them the home-turf advantage) a week from Tuesday (be fairly specific about the place and date). If that day doesn't work, when is best for you?

Sample email to anyone to get the conversation started:

Dear _____,

As a volunteer member of the Capital Campaign Council, I often get to meet with other donors of the _____ to share information about our priorities.

My position on this Council gives me access to a real depth of information about _____, and puts me in a lucky position to build a conduit between you and _____.

I got involved ____ years ago when _____ (for example, I attended classes, when I knew someone who needed these

services, a family member was helped). I am writing to see if I could meet with you and have an opportunity to share my enthusiasm. More importantly, I would like to hear your thoughts on _____
_'s future direction.

Please let me know if you would be willing to talk by phone or meet in person.

Cultivation Plan

If you are working on a major campaign with a longer timeline, you really should have what we in the business call a "Cultivation Plan." You already know that the timeline is two years or so. However, you're probably not aware that the average major gift takes 18 months to close. This is not a one-and-done meeting. This process takes several calls and several meetings. You might start with a prospect you've never met and end up as the greatest of friends.

Just as you cultivate a friendship over time, a cultivation plan allows you to cultivate the donation over time. Your first meeting may be a lunch with the CEO, followed by a tour of the organization. You might then invite the prospect to an event hosted by the non-profit such as the annual gala or Lunch & Learn. Slowly, over time, you will introduce the prospect to the campaign and make the ask, typically with someone from the institution at that meeting. All of these steps and meetings were loosely planned in advance, that's the cultivation plan.

Share your enthusiasm for the cause with as many people

as possible. You can even think of a cultivation plan for everyone you meet, not to get a donation, but to connect them to the organization. Just do what comes naturally, share your passion for a good cause.

The song *"Feel This Moment" (2012)*, by Pitbull and featuring Christina Aguilera, included the lyrics:

*"Ask for money, and get advice.
Ask for advice, get money twice."*
—Pitbull

8

WHO, WHAT, WHEN, WHERE, WHY AND NOW HOW

AT THIS POINT, YOU KNOW WHY YOU'RE GOING to ask, who you're going to ask, when you're going to ask, where you're going to ask, and what you're going to ask. However, you might not know exactly *how* you're going to ask. Knowing the "how" should relieve whatever tiny kernel of anxiety you have left.

All your hard work up until this point is about to pay off. The demographics of the prospect will allow you to tailor the ask to the audience. The "how" for a millennial won't work for the baby boomers and vice versa. Make sure you adjust your language and approach based on the information you've gathered about the prospect. Also, knowing the amount of the ask informs how you will ask. What works for a $25 annual gift differs substantially from what is involved in an ask for $5,000 to $25,000 which, in turn, differs from a $100,000 to $1,000,000 ask.

The easiest and most important rule to remember for any mid to large ask is make sure you have a written handout to legitimize the ask. Give the prospective donor information about what you are requesting (if it is money, make sure to include how much); why the donation is needed (case for support); how it will impact the community; and when it is needed. That can be a letter or another document such as the pledge form below.

STEINWAY
The Next Stage for Mason

Thank you for investing in our students!

Pledge of Support

Contact Name(s) _____

Acknowledgement Name *as will appear in print* _____

Mailing Address _____

Phone _____ E-mail _____

☐ **Individual purchase of one (or more) Steinway grand pianos –** **$75,000 each** (Pledges can be paid over a period of 10 years – $7,500 annually)

☐ *88 Key Circle* – purchase of one or more keys on a Steinway grand piano – **$1,000 per key** (Pledges can be paid over a period of 5 years – $200 annually)

☐ **Group purchase of a Steinway grand piano – $75,000 each** (Pledges can be paid over a period of 10 years – $7,500 annually) *No limit to the number of persons in a group*

☐ Participation in *Steinway ~ The Next Stage for Mason* – **under $1,000**

Please indicate below how you wish to fulfill your pledge:
☐ My/Our gifts will be completed over ____ years, beginning on *(month/day)* _____ of *(year)* _____

YEAR	AMOUNT	YEAR	AMOUNT	YEAR	AMOUNT	YEAR	AMOUNT	YEAR	AMOUNT
Year 1		Year 3		Year 5		Year 7		Year 9	
Year 2		Year 4		Year 6		Year 8		Year 10	

☐ Check is enclosed (make checks payable to: "GMU Foundation/Steinway Initiative")

☐ Charge my credit card: ☐ Visa   ☐ Master Card   ☐ AMEX

Account Number _____

Name *(as it appears on card)* _____

Exp. Date _____ Signature _____

For more information regarding *Steinway ~ The Next Stage for Mason*, please contact:

It can be delivered at the meeting or even sent as a follow-up confirmation of your conversation. Just make sure that you have it, and it matches the information you are about to deliver in your face-to-face meeting.

Designed by Judson Design for Dress for Success Houston, this two-sided "Fact Card" is housed at the front desk and given to every potential donor or volunteer who walks in the building.

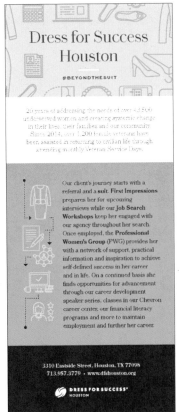

If your organization has a particularly good website, make sure to include the link in your written documents and any email correspondence. You could also use the site as part of your presentation. Nurturingmindsinafrica. org has a great video about the organization and why you should give right on the homepage. It's like they're doing the work for you!

Your Last Option as a First Step

The most common reason someone gives is their belief in the organization through personal experience. Sometimes the reason is that someone is seeking acceptance in a community among peers. Often, it depends on who asks or the timing.

Once in awhile, timing demands that a really good fundraising letter is absolutely necessary as a first step. Sometimes, you just won't be able to see the person face to face or schedule a call because you can't get past the gatekeepers. However, you have the correct address.

Make sure the letter follows all the same rules as your in-person ask and the recipient knows up front they are being asked for a gift. If it is a substantial ask, write a personal, handwritten note on the formal letter, as well. Give the prospect your personal cell phone number or email address for follow-up.

Dear _____,

I've rediscovered something.

A good many letters appealing for charitable funds end up in the wastebasket because they think that such appeals are really intended for someone else, and especially for people who give big gifts.

Before you toss this one away, will you think with me

for a minute about whether and why you might spare a few dollars?

You see, if most of our community will respond to this letter to the extent of even a couple of dollars, it will make a world of difference—and do a world of good!

Of course, we need large gifts, indeed must have them, and is exceedingly grateful for them. But large numbers of small gifts can match smaller numbers of large gifts and thus can do great work.

They can buy _____, they can help _____, they can build _____ in the community.

Now that you've read this far, don't toss this letter away. Put it with your monthly bills, and when you start writing checks for the mortgage, water, electricity, write one more for us, even if it's a small one.

Please use the enclosed envelope. And be assured of warmest thanks—from those who will benefit, and from all of us volunteers.

Sincerely,

In Writing or In Person:
1. Be personal.
2. Be specific.
3. Listen.
4. Ask for a specific amount. You want to give the prospective donor something to which she can react.
5. Don't rush the ask. If it doesn't seem like a natural part of the conversation, it's likely too soon.
6. Aim high. Donors will respond to your ambitions.

7. Tailor your language to your prospect. You may not want to make it sound like you are asking for an order. Consider softening your approach with: "Would you be comfortable if I talked with you about a commitment of $x to _____to support_____?" Try to avoid complicated and convoluted language in your ask and your written documents.
8. Leave with an agreement on the next steps: Who is doing what? What is needed by the prospective donor to continue the conversation or make a decision?
9. Don't promise what you can't deliver, tempting though it may be.
10. Express gratitude

Think about the key points you want to emphasize.

All of the information should be second nature to you because you practiced, practiced, practiced and researched, researched, researched. You are ready, ready, ready.

Putting thought into the ask beforehand increases the chances for success and tears down obstacles. However, you will have to feel your way through the meeting to determine when to say what. It's a skill you'll develop over time if you actually listen to your prospect during the meeting.

When in doubt, ask yourself, if I were this donor:
• What would I expect to hear?
• What would I want to hear?
• Where would I want to meet?
• And if you were this donor, what would you say in response to an ask?

Let's go through it step by step.

Assume you are meeting a woman in her 60s at her office. She's a partner in a law firm who supports local education for disenfranchised youth. You are asking for money to support building a youth center with job training near her office. She's the perfect fit.

You've done your research and know she hasn't made a major gift recently, her kids are all out of the house and successful in their own right, and she has no plans for retirement in the near future. Knowing the cause is a good fit and based on her position and circumstances, you decide to ask for the $1,000,000 naming rights to the building.

Though you do have a relationship with her, you know it's best to have someone from the non-profit with you for the ask. Great thinking! Two people asking is more effective when done right. It gives one a chance to talk and the other to listen, or for you both to listen when your prospect is speaking. You should never make the prospect feel outnumbered. The other representative is there to make her feel important and worthy of the extra attention.

You are guided into the office and the two of you introduce yourselves. Your prospect rushes you into your seats and looks annoyed that you both showed up. Take your cue from her, and say something along the lines of:

"Thank you so much for taking the time to meet with us today, we know how busy you are and promise not to take up too much of your time. I just really wanted you to meet the person whose vision is leading this campaign."

Now, stop, don't talk. Let the other person talk. Listen

to the conversation they are having. Notice how the prospect's demeanor has changed. She looks more relaxed, looks interested in the project. She wants to hear more about the youth your organization serves and how the building will help them. They turn it over to you.

You begin speaking the words you practiced a thousand times. They don't sound rehearsed, they sound like a natural part of the conversation. You stop to let your prospect ask a question. It leads naturally to your saying, "As your office overlooks the very spot the building will be and you're known as an advocate for education, naturally, we wanted to offer you the $1,000,000 naming rights." You slide the written documents over to her and remain silent.

Listen. Observe. See what she's saying with her body language. Does she balk or stiffen? Nod her head or shake it? Does she remain silent for an excruciating amount of time?

The most common reason someone goes silent is they were surprised that the meeting was about giving to an organization. Never, never surprise the donor by saying that you just want to have coffee when in fact the meeting is to talk about a very worthy cause.

Eventually, she'll say she needs to discuss it with a few people. This is a good sign. You didn't seriously think she would say yes to a million dollar ask on the spot, did you? Of course not!

Before you leave, create a sense of urgency. There are so many good causes out there, so many ways to spread the philanthropic dollars. You want yours to rise to the top, but you also want those you ask to give sooner rather than later. Remind her that there is a deadline for the naming gift. If you have a corporate matching sponsor, this can create a sense of urgency, as well.

Always leave the conversation knowing that you and the prospective donor understand why you made the call or visit; you made it to ask for a gift. The most common reason that someone doesn't give to your campaign? The person was not asked directly and/or didn't realize she was being asked.

Before you leave, determine what the next step should be. Always leave a meeting with a game plan as to what to do next. Write it down and put it on the calendar.

"Our great weakness lies in giving up. The most certain way to succeed is always to try just one more time."

—Thomas Edison

9

IT'S NOT OVER UNTIL IT'S OVER (AND IT'S NEVER OVER)

THIS IS ONE OF THOSE TIMES IN LIFE WHEN LESS IS not more. When you leave the meeting, you want your prospect to know why you were there, what your cause is about, and what will happen next. It bears repeating, always leave a meeting with a game plan as to what to do next. Write it down and put it on the calendar. Most importantly, whether you received a yes, no, or I'll-have-to-think-about-it, always leave the meeting with a smile and thank-you-for-your-time.

Speaking of thank yous, a little advice: When you book the meeting, start writing your thank you note. This will be a physical card, written in your handwriting. Get some notecards or stationery made with your name and board members listed and use that. (Email is great, but getting something in the mail these days is unusual and quite effective.) It will include personal information from the meeting, so you can't finish it until later, but you can start it and carry it with you to the meeting. Address and stamp the envelope ahead of time. Put all this in your car or briefcase. As soon as you leave the meeting, while all is fresh, finish the note and drop it in the mail.

This is the thank you note for taking the meeting, so everyone you meet, regardless of response, gets one. If the prospect has turned into a donor, feel free to thank them for their generosity of both time and support. This is a touch that will set you apart, this is one of those things that can turn a no into a yes. At the very least, they won't start avoiding you when you run into each other at another organization's fundraiser!

FOLLOW UP THE YES

After your initial thank you note, you'll want to let your organization know about your success and next steps. You might have a plan in place to have the CEO meet with major donors at a press event or a fun party. Your donor might need to discuss distributing the gift over several years. Maybe the donor just wants to meet the people they are helping. You need to pass along all of that information.

Plus, it's fun to share your success with others and celebrate those early wins, no matter how large or small. Tell your fellow board members about your victories. Surround yourself with fellow supporters of the cause. Studies show we tend to adopt the goals and energy of the people around us. Enthusiasm is contagious!

> ELOISE DUNN BRICE
>
> Dear Volunteer,
> What you have done in nothing
> short of amazing. You made this
> goal happen – moreover you changed
> the lives of 30 students. Thank you!
> Elise

SAMPLE THANK YOU NOTES –

Know how you love to get thank you notes? Well, so do donors. They want simple ones that just express gratitude. And it's fun to say thank you as well as hear it.

Dear _____,
This is just a note to say thank you for your generosity and vision in making a gift to _____. I am grateful, but, moreover, the many who will benefit from your support have better lives.
Sincerely,

OR

Dear _____,
Yesterday, I met some of the recipients of your scholarship and was touched, impressed, and thankful for your generosity. How wonderful to see that they will now be able to finish high school and think about a better life with more education.

You can even get others to write thank you notes for you.

You might have to organize this—for students it takes free pizza, some note cards, and pens. However, their notes can be simple. It can be a simple thank you that they craft on their own, from their hearts.

To make it more fun, corral your fellow volunteers and have a joint thank you writing party.

FOLLOW UP THE POLITE MAYBE

Keep in touch with donors and prospects who seemed interested but uncommitted. You'll have more than a few of these. It's best to ask open-ended questions to determine real level of interest and next steps. If you determine a prospect is really not interested, best for all if you know definitively and can plan accordingly. Usually it's a matter of taking him or her off the list, but sometimes it's just a matter of waiting for the right timing to reopen the conversation. Avoid wasting time and energy on issues you cannot change but don't lock the door.

You will leave some meetings with a "no," or its polite equivalent. Don't take it personally, it wasn't you. You can't give money to every cause and neither can your prospects. Remember, this was built into your gift table, your calculations on how to reach your goal. You're asking four prospects to get one yes. It's to be expected.

However, an initial "no" can turn into a surprise "yes" months or years down the road.

One of my mentors has told me a story about a donor who ended up giving $15M to his non-profit after years of seemingly nothing. It started with years of clandestine meetings with lawyers who would not reveal the client's name, years of silence during an economic downturn, and then lo and behold the donor emerged with a big gift for the very purpose originally discussed.

These surprise successes are only possible when you know how to deal with rejection graciously and realize that "no" is just a temporary set-back on the path to success.

FOLLOW UP THE NO

Don't stew about any declinations. You did the right thing by asking. Write a letter or note of thanks to the one you asked, and move on (you should have already done this immediately following your meeting).

If you think it was just a matter of timing, keep in contact with the potential donor throughout the next year. Leave the door open. Keep your relationship strong without pushing. We have all heard volunteer fundraisers who say their friends are crossing the street rather than greeting them by the end. Don't let that be you. You are just keeping the cause alive without pressure.

You'd be forgiven if you assumed the objections are pretty evenly distributed, but the distribution looks more like this:

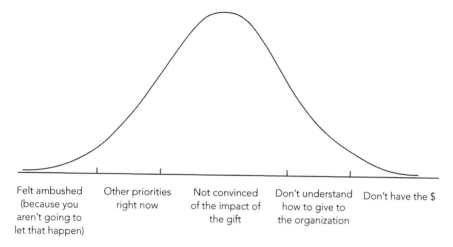

Felt ambushed (because you aren't going to let that happen) • Other priorities right now • Not convinced of the impact of the gift • Don't understand how to give to the organization • Don't have the $

You'll be able to deal with some objections right away, but some might need more time or someone else to deal with them. Here's a list of common objections you might hear, what they actually mean, and what you should do about them.

"Call me back in a month."

This can mean no interest or bad timing. Just put it on your calendar to call back in a month. Most volunteers wait two or three, that is a deal killer because it signals to the potential donor the this is not important. We follow through with the things that are important in life.

"My plate is full, I have many other charities I support."

Congratulate them on what they are doing for others. Ask for a suggestion of someone they know who might be interested in your organization. Those who are donors have friends who are donors. They just do.

"Can you give me more details?"

Ask some specific questions to know exactly what the donor means. Do they have questions about the purpose of the organization? Do they wonder who is served in the community? Do they know of similar or competing services in the community? Or do they wonder what money is needed and who else has already given?

Make sure each donor is given written collateral. It's entirely common to think you have explained something well, but the prospective donor walked away with some confusion or a different understanding. They may wonder how much was the request? What would it really help? When does the organization need it?

So, write it down for others. Either bring it with you for the meeting or send afterward with a note.

"I can give half of what you are asking."

Beyond just an enthusiastic thank you, give him a pledge form. Ask if you can share the amount given to inspire the next donor (because it will).

"I give to your main initiatives."

Try not to bristle at the idea of not wanting to help with this campaign. Donors often see organizations as fighting to capture their treasure.

Ghosting (AKA Radio Silence)

Move on. Either you aren't the right person to solicit the gift or the project isn't of any interest. Did I say move on? I mean move on after you have made four solid attempts.

When you are consistently hitting a brick wall:

Consider surveying your prospects rather than asking them for money. Ask questions such as:

1-Do you understand the organization? Its mission and values?

2-Do you have any personal connection with the organization?

3-Do you think this organization is important to the community? (why or why not)

4-Does our organization do a good job of differentiating itself from similar non-profits in the area?

5-What are the non-profits?

Today's technology makes surveying your prospects as easy as sending an email.

At some point, you will be faced with a "Not my cup of tea, darling" sort of response. Be gracious. Be grateful. Follow up with a thank you note regardless.

You, too, might have to learn to deliver the polite no. I asked a very community minded friend why she avoided fundraising. She said it was because everyone she asked then asked her for a gift for their charities. She's right. This does happen. You have to be careful how you ask. The best solution is to be upfront with those you solicit, saying that you are focusing all your current giving on the organization where you are on the volunteer board.

MOVING FORWARD

Stewardship of all your donors and prospects is important. The most common reason someone gives is belief in the organization through personal experience. Whether you handle it as a volunteer or ask the paid staff to do so, it must be done to ensure future engagement.

Plan an activity with them and your fellow volunteers. Maybe it is time with the recipients of their largess and giving (kids, patients, elderly). Maybe it's a cocktail party or a garden party. Donors want to know that they made a good choice, that you led them in the right direction. Nothing is as powerful as meeting the people they have helped.

Also, put reminders in your calendar to let your prospects and donors know about progress and good news. Ongoing information about how the gift is being used and testimonials of those helped are tangible progress of the organization.

When you see the donors next time, thank them again.

If you are a fundraising volunteer repeater then go to those donors again. "You have been very generous to _____, have you considered increasing your annual gift?

And with some it might even make sense to ask them if they have considered _____in their estate plans.

To do this, of course, you'll have to track your progress. Analytics are everywhere, data driven decisions are clearly the hot topic. But there is also good old fashioned record keeping that will help you and help your successors.

Keep a record of everyone you solicited. You can even do it right on your gift table (see example below). Keep a note of the conversation (one or two sentences will do it) because you will forget once the campaign is in full swing, and you will want a way to hand off information quickly. It is best to do you quick summary right after your conversation.

Set up a system to update the gift table as you progress. The mere thought of success can also be a potent motivating force for some. This is why we construct cardboard thermometers or set up a webpage that shows how close we are to a goal. People sometimes kick in money for the simple joy of seeing the mercury move a little higher. Use it.

Name of person asked	Yes, Maybe, No	Conversation highlights	Other info	Follow-up needed
Jane Smith (XXX) XXX-XXXX	Maybe	Needs more info about programs	Daughter graduating this year	Send info sheet and call Jan. 4
Mike Edwards mike@edwards.com	YES	Huge Supporter!	Loves the newsletter	Send TY note and invite to kick-off event

"Never give up, for that is just the place and time that the tide will turn."

—Harriet Beecher Stowe

CONCLUSION AND LESSONS LEARNED

LESSON ONE
The majority of fundraising is sharing your enthusiasm for the mission.

LESSON TWO
Your organization will set you up for success, however you define it, by providing documents, timelines, gift tables, and a clear definition of the type of campaign being launched and your role in the fundraising.

LESSON THREE
If you need help or support, check your Ghostbuster List and just ask!

LESSON FOUR
Be the first to give. You'll get practice and experience in giving to this kind of campaign. You'll also feel better when it's time to ask someone else to give, too!

LESSON FIVE
Know exactly why the organization is launching the campaign and be specific about who the funds will be helping and how.

LESSON SIX
Practice makes difficult things easier and easy things second nature, so practice your fear away.

LESSON SEVEN
Start your outreach with a plan based on your timeline that will guarantee you early wins. If all else fails, just start starting.

LESSON EIGHT
Knowledge is power: know your prospect, so you can know the ask.

LESSON NINE
Don't be afraid to talk about money up front, and don't surprise your prospect with the ask. A "no" is not the end of the world, but an annoyed prospect might write you off for good.

LESSON TEN
Never take a "no" personally. It could just be a matter of other priorities or timing. Always take a "yes" personally! You have spent your time well and your cause is worthy.

You are now the best of the best. You represent an organization that is helping members of your community or the world become better in some way. Your success comes from spreading the word, retaining your enthusiasm for the mission, and, of course, meeting your goal. Congratulations! Now, go have a Samoa!

Made in the USA
Las Vegas, NV
14 March 2023

69063651R00064